JACKIE

T&J

Published by TAJ Books International LLC 2014
5501 Kincross Lane
Charlotte, North Carolina, USA
28277

www.tajbooks.com
www.tajminibooks.com

All notations of errors or omissions (author inquiries, permissions) concerning the content of this book should be addressed to info@tajbooks.com. The publishers wish to thank Abbie Rowe, National Park Service/John Fitzgerald Kennedy Library, Boston.

ISBN 978-1-84406-269-0

Printed in China
1 2 3 4 5 18 17 16 15 14

Jackie

T&J

BY KATHRYN DIXON

JACKIE

T he woman so famous that she is known today the world over by the simple appellation "Jackie" was born Jacqueline Lee Bouvier on July 28, 1929, in Southampton, New York, to the Wall Street stockbroker John "Black Jack" Bouvier and Janet Norton Lee. She was the couple's first-born child. Four years later, her sister Caroline Lee Bouvier was born. Her parents would divorce in 1940. Little did she—or anyone else for that matter—anticipate the important role she would play on the world stage as an adult.

1934, aged four years old

JACKIE

Before her parents' divorce in 1940, Jackie and Lee's childhood summers were spent in East Hampton, New York, at Lasata, the summer home of her paternal grandparents. Her father, known as "Black Jack" as much for his extravagant lifestyle as for his exotic dark looks, contributed to the breakup of the marriage through his excessive drinking, gambling, and carousing with women other than his wife. He never remarried. Jackie adored him regardless. It is speculated that her acceptance of her father's philandering made it easier for her to handle her husband's with the magnanimity that she did.

1935, with her parents at the Southampton Riding and Hunt Club on Long Island, New York

JACKIE

By the age of 11, Jackie was an accomplished equestrienne. Reading was also a favorite pastime. Her elementary school years were spent at Miss Chapin's School in Manhattan where the family lived on Park Avenue. Her mother remarried in 1942 to Hugh Auchincloss. With the marriage, Jackie's family expanded to include three stepsiblings—Yusha, Nina, and Tommy—soon to be joined by half-siblings, Janet and James. Jackie's high school years were spent at Miss Porter's school for girls in Connecticut. She attended Vassar, but graduated from George Washington University in 1951 after spending her junior year in Paris, France.

c. 1946, The Auchincloss Family, from back, L-R: Jacqueline Bouvier, Yusha Auchincloss, Nina Auchincloss, Lee Bouvier, Janet Auchincloss (holding baby Janet Auchincloss), Tommy Auchincloss, Hugh D. Auchincloss

JACKIE

J ackie started her first job in the fall of 1951 as the "Inquiring Camera Girl" for the *Washington Times-Herald* newspaper. She spent her day out and about in Washington, DC, taking pictures of the people she encountered on the street and asking them questions about the hot topics of the day. Her newspaper column was based on their answers and of course included their photos. During this time, Jackie met John F. Kennedy, then a congressman who would soon be elected a Senator from Massachusetts.

1953, photographed in her role as the "Inquiring Camera Girl" for the Washington Times-Herald *newspaper*

JACKIE

The new Senator and Mrs. John Kennedy had been introduced by a mutual friend, journalist Charles Bartlett, at a dinner part in May 1952. Little more than a year later, after becoming engaged on 25 June 1953, Jackie and Jack Kennedy were married on 12 September 1953 at St. Mary's Church in Newport, Rhode Island. The wedding was officiated by Boston's Archbishop Cushing with nearly 700 guests in attendance. The reception was held at nearby Hammersmith Farm, the Auchincloss summer home. Over 1,200 guests joined in the celebration!

1953, her bridal portrait

JACKIE

J ackie's formidable style was evident in her choice of wedding dress. Ann Lowe, a black designer and dressmaker in Manhattan, is responsble for the creation. Amazingly, 10 days before the wedding, a water line broke in Ms. Lowe's studio, totally ruinng Jackie's dress and all 10 pink bridesmaids' dresses. Ms. Lowe worked unceasingly to recreate all of the dresses in time for the wedding. Jackie's off-the-shoulder dress required 50 yards of ivory silk taffeta. The dress is currently on display at the John F. Kennedy Presidential Library and Museum in Boston, Massachusetts.

1953, on her wedding day, being helped by the groomsmen

Hugh Auchincloss, Jackie's stepfather, walked her down the aisle even though her father was present at the wedding. The couple honeymooned in Mexico before returning home to Washington, DC. The first years of their marriage were marred by Jack Kennedy's two spinal surgeries to correct debilitating football and wartime injuries as well as by a miscarriage for the couple. Making matters worse, Jack Kennedy also suffered from Addison's disease, a disorder in which the body produces insufficient amounts of certain adrenal gland hormones. Symptoms include pain in the lower back, muscle and joint pain, and muscle weakness and fatigue. Although his diagnosis was made in the 1940s, it was not publicly known until after the 1960 US presidential election.

1953, on her wedding day, preparing to throw her bouquet

JACKIE

To distract her husband from his lack of mobility during his recoveries from back surgery, Jackie encouraged him to write *Profiles in Courage*. The Pulitzer Prize–winning book tells the stories of eight US senators throughout the Senate's history who risked their careers to fight for what they believed in. The book was published in 1955 and won the Pulizer Prize for history in 1957. They had a second reason to celebrate that year when their first child Caroline was born. Soon, Jackie and Jack would be busy campaigning across the country in hopes that Jack could capture the Democratic nomination and ultimately the presidency in November 1960.

*1954, with her husband as he enters the hospital for
spinal surgery*

JACKIE

Just two-and-a-half weeks after her husband beat Richard Nixon by a nose in the 1960 presidential election, Jackie gave birth to their second child, John F. Kennedy, Jr. Because she was pregnant during most of the campaign and unable to travel, Jackie contributed by answering letters, taping TV commercials, giving interviews, and writing a weekly newspaper column that was called "Campaign Wife." Even for those who didn't agree with her husband's politics, most Americans warmly applauded the first family with young children to inhabit the White House in many years.

*20 January 1961, the new First Lady listens intently to
her husband's Inaugural Address*

JACKIE

On a very cold 20 January 1961, Jackie watched as her husband took the oath of office to become the nation's 35th president. At the age of 31, Jackie was America's new First Lady and one of the youngest in the nation's history. Jackie's White House legacy extends from restoring the White House itself to raising the style and cuisine quotient of State dinners to championing the arts and culture in US society to representing the nation with unprecedented good taste in both her appearance and her manner. Her first priorities, however, were to be a good wife to her husband and a good mother to her children.

1961, arriving at yet another Inaugural ball

JACKIE

On Inauguration Day, Jackie wore a wool coat and pillbox hat designed by her favorite designer, Oleg Cassini, who also created her long white satin gown for the evening's festivities. Allegedly, she detested hats of any kind and only grudgingly agreed to wear it. Doing so, however, caused an overnight sensation in the millinery shops across America. This was just the first of many occasions on which Jackie wowed the public with her style and verve. Soon, she would be winning over the Parisians, famous for *haute couture*, when she visited with her husband in May 1961.

Inauguration Day 1961, President and Mrs. Kennedy celebrate the day

JACKIE

As First Lady, Jackie invited artists, writers, scientists, poets, and musicians to mingle with politicians, diplomats, and statesmen at White House special events and dinners. But the First Couple were often out on the town as well. Jackie charmed everyone she met, a talent particularly valuable when she met with formidable foreign diplomats and their wives, such as the Soviet leader Nikita Khrushchev and his wife, Nina. In many respects, Jackie was America's No. 1 secret weapon in the war of public opinion and personality.

1961, the Kennedys enroute to a private party

JACKIE

Not only was Jackie's mission to make the White House a building that the country could be proud of, she wanted to make it a home for her family. She had the third-floor sun porch enclosed to make a kindergarten for Caroline and John and invited 12 to 15 other children to attend. School began promptly at 9:30am Monday through Friday. Meanwhile, she threw herself wholeheartedly into the project of restoring the public rooms of the White House and ensuring that the building would be preserved as a national treasure for its lifetime. To do so, she established a Fine Arts Committee and created the post of White House curator.

1961, holding a silver pitcher presented as a gift for the White House by James Hoban Alexander

JACKIE

In addition to managing the White House restoration project, accompanying her husband around the world, and entertaining foreign dignitaries, Jackie had numerous official events to attend on her own. One such event was the christening of the ballistic missile submarine *USS Lafayette*. Soon, she would be off to India with her sister, Lee, on a goodwill tour where she would be greeted by India's Prime Minister Jawaharlal Nehru and his daughter, Indira Ghandi.

1962, christening the USS Lafayette

JACKIE

The culmination of the White House restoration project—paid for in part by proceeds from the first ever White House guidebook, also initiated by Jackie—was a tour led by the First Lady and televised by CBS in February 1962. Eighty million Americans tuned in. Jackie was awarded an honorary Emmy for her participation in the program. After the restoration was complete, art and furniture from around the United States graced the halls of the White House where it remains today. Many of the pieces had belonged to former presidents and their families.

*1962, starring in the White House tour after the renovation
and refurbishment she instigated*

JACKIE

J ohn Kenneth Galbraith, the US Ambassador to India at the time, encouraged Jackie to visit India and Pakistan on a goodwill tour in May 1962. Photojournalists documented every move that Jackie and her sister, Lee Radziwill, made, and the worldwide publicity they received was staggering. While in Pakistan Jackie rode a camel, and in India, she rode an elephant. As a welcoming gesture, the Pakistani President Ayub Khan gave Jackie a horse named Sardar. In reciprocation for her visit, Khan came to Washington later that same year.

1962, in India with her sister, Lee

JACKIE

Enthralled by the beauty of the Taj Mahal, Jackie visited the monument twice: once in the morning and again in the moonlight. She toured a textile factory, watched a polo match in Jaipur, and visited a children's hospital. LIFE magazine estimated Jackie wore 22 different outfits during her trip, many of which were exquisitely colorful in keeping with the bright hues of India. She was said to have changed her outfit five times in one day when in New Delhi! But her appeal was not only visual. Her intellect was noticeable to everyone she came in contact with and her language skills were out of the ordinary; both made her an outstanding emissary for her country.

1962, having a bindi, which signifies marriage, placed on her forehead in Jaipur during her state trip to India

JACKIE

Representing the US on a goodwill trip to Paris, Vienna, and Greece—this time with her husband—Jackie made an equally memorable impression. Clark Clifford, a respected lawyer and advisor to the Kennedy administration, wrote her the following once she had returned from her journey: "Once in a great while, an individual will capture the imagination of people all over the world. You have done this; and what is more important, through your graciousness and tact, you have transformed this rare accomplishment into an incredibly important asset to this nation."

1962, in front of the Taj Mahal in Agra, India

JACKIE

Mount Vernon, the home of George Washington, was the site of the state dinner in the summer of 1961 that honored the President of Pakistan, Mohammed Ayub Khan. As befitting a true Southern occasion, the First Lady chose to serve mint juleps on the piazza overlooking the Potomac. The dinner also was served out of doors, under a tent on the lawn. The tent was decorated by Tiffany & Co. Also, as is true of many an outdoor Southern event, the venue was swarming with mosquitos. Last minute mosquito bombs did the trick, but overzealous corpsmen wielding the poison also sprayed the elegant food that had been prepared for the evening. After some vigorous taste testing that left no one gagging or ill, the meal was on!

1961, at the State Dinner in Honor of President Mohammad Ayub Khan of Pakistan held at Mount Vernon, seated beside the honoree

JACKIE

B eginning in February 1961, less than two weeks after Jack Kennedy was sworn into office as president, Jack and Jackie took a lease on a horse farm near Middleburg, Virginia. In the saddle by the age of one, Jackie adored being an equestrienne and was quite an accomplished one at that. The farm called Glen-Ora was home to Jackie, Jack, Caroline, and John on many weekends. It was at Glen-Ora that she hosted the Pakistani President Ayub Kahn when he visited the US in the fall of 1962. The horse he gave her when she visited Pakistan on her goodwill tour the previous year was stabled at Glen-Ora.

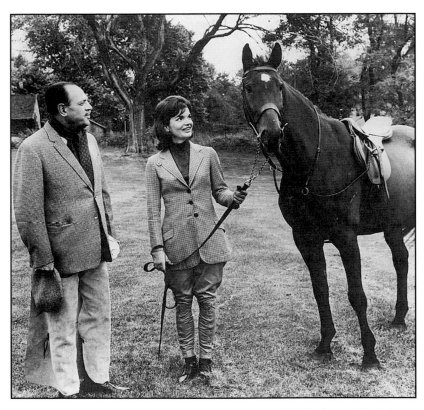

1962, with Pakistani President Ayub Khan in Middleburg, Virginia, holding the reins to Sardar, the bay gelding he had given her a year earlier

JACKIE

While she lived in the White House, Jackie hunted with the Orange County (Virginia) Hunt, one of the most prestigious hunt clubs in America. Jackie and Jack loved Virginia horse country so much that they bought almost 40 acres near Atoka to build their own home, Wexford, which they designed themselves. They had barely moved into their new weekend home when President Kennedy was shot. Although the first family only visited Wexford on two occasions before the president's death, home movies captured this special place in their hearts. Jackie sold the house in 1964.

1962, riding her horse Ninbrano, Jackie clears a hurdle at the Loudoun Hunt horse show in Leesburg, Virginia

JACKIE

F ox hunting and the Virginia countryside held tremendous appeal for Jackie throughout her life. Jackie returned to the Middleburg area in the mid-1980s where she rented a small, unpretentious clapboard cottage that she used each spring and fall until 1993, just prior to her death. At a Sotheby's auction in 1996, one of her cracked and well-worn saddles sold for $90,500, a great deal more than it was worth, but surely meriting the value placed on it by the purchaser when considered in historical and sentimental terms. Jackie passed on her love of horses to her young daughter, Caroline, whose pony Macaroni grazed on the White House lawn.

1962, at the Apple Barrel pony rally in Halfway,
Virginia, where she is obviously a person of
interest to the youg boys next to her

JACKIE

During her 1,000-day tenure in the White House, Jackie was a devoted advocate of all things cultural. Jackie especially loved literature and poetry and did so from a young age. She always had her nose in a book. As a high school senior, her original cartoon series published in the school paper won her the graduating award for literature. In 1951, out of 1,280 entrants, she won *Vogue* magazine's Prix de Paris contest with her submission of an original theme for an entire issue, illustrations, articles, layout and design, as well as an advertising campaign that supported the issue's theme. Her mother did not want her to leave the country—the winner spent half a year in New York City and the other half in Paris—so she had to turn down the prize.

1962, exiting the National Theater in Washington, DC, with President Kennedy

49

JACKIE

Jackie encouraged her husband to invite numerous artists from all the cultural disciplines to attend the inauguration as a symbolic gesture of the Kennedy administration's intended goal of supporting the arts. At one time Jackie had expressed aspirations of writing a novel, but life intervened and instead she assumed the role of coordinating editor for her husband's Pulitzer Prize-winning book, *Profiles in Courage*, and researched historical examples and quotations to be used in his speeches. Jackie's command of languages—French, Italian, and Spanish—allowed her to communicate directly with many non-English speakers. Her ability to do so endeared her to many and reinforced just what an asset she was to her country.

1962, crossing the White House lawn

JACKIE

Oleg Cassini was her primary designer but she also wore clothes designed by the fashion houses of Chanel, Givenchy, and Dior. Numerous elements of her wardrobe were knocked off by commercial clothing manufacturers; as a result, her style could be worn and enjoyed by any woman who chose to emulate it. She chose a pink suit in various iterations, including sadly on her visit to Dallas, and it was a stellar example of classic chic but with her unique touch of pizzazz. Jackie loved pearls and a triple-strand faux pearl necklace graced her neck most often while she was First Lady. It is believed that the necklace was designed by Coco Chanel and given to Jackie by her mother, Janet Auchincloss.

October 1962, deplaning in NYC where she was to receive a citation for her contribution to culture and the arts from New York University's Institute of Fine Arts

JACKIE

J ackie, Jack, Caroline, and John spent many a relaxing day at Jack's parents' home in Palm Beach, Florida. Jack also recuperated from his back surgeries in 1954 and 1955 in Palm Beach, where he wrote *Profiles in Courage*. After the 1960 election, Jackie and Jack retreated to the Palm Beach compound to unwind and prepare for the challenging days that surely faced them as president and first lady. And fatefully, Jack would spend the November days just before his trip to Dallas in 1963 at the Palm Beach house, near where he was speaking in Miami and Tampa. He also visited Cape Canaveral at this time. It would be renamed the Kennedy Space Center after his death.

Easter 1963 at President Kennedy's parents' home in Palm Beach, Florida

JACKIE

H yannis Port, Massachusetts, not far from the Kennedy clan's hometown of Boston, was a welcome haven for Jackie and Jack and their children. Joe and Rose Kennedy began vacationing in Hyannis Port in 1926. The wide expanse of lawn between their home and the Atlantic Ocean fielded many a touch football game as the large Kennedy family congregated there over the years. Jack and Jackie bought a house close by in 1956. Jackie and Caroline were photographed for a pre-election photo spread published in LIFE magazine at their home in Hyannis Port, and a pregnant Jackie watched the televised 1960 Kennedy-Nixon debate from there as well.

1963, the Kennedy family in Hyannis Port, Massachusetts

Not until November 1961 did Jackie and the children first visit Camp David, the presidential retreat in the Catoctin Mountains of western Maryland not far from Washington, DC. A recreation field near the house was turned into a riding ring for Caroline. When not being used for that purpose, it served as the presidential helicopter's landing pad. During the Cuban Missile Crisis in 1962, if Jackie and the children had been sent away for safety, it would likely have been to Camp David, which houses a bomb shelter.

1963, at Camp David admiring Caroline astride her pony

K enneth, called the first celebrity hairdresser, styled Jackie's hair from 1954 to 1986 and is responsible for her early 1960s bouffant hairstyle, emulated by so many women around the world. Ironically, another Kenneth client was Marilyn Monroe, rumored to have had an affair with Jack Kennedy in the year prior to her death in August 1962. Audrey Hepburn, another fabulous style icon of the early 1960s, also shared Kenneth's salon chair. Kenneth styled Jackie's hair just before she accompanied her husband on his fateful trip to Dallas on 22 November 1963.

13 November 1963, President and Mrs. Kennedy regard the performance of the Black Watch Tattoo on the South Lawn of the White House

JACKIE

A though unknown at the time, Jackie's role as First Lady went far beyond the arts, entertaining, and maintaining a stylish appearance. During the Cuban Missile Crisis in 1962, although many high-ranking officials were evacuated from Washington, DC, Jackie remained at her husband's side and was aware of each top-secret move made by the US and the Soviet Union. She subtly supported the civil rights movement by integrating the White House kindergarten, and after her husband's assassination she wrote to Soviet Premier Nikita Khrushchev imploring him to stay committed to nuclear arms reduction. She believed the 1963 Nuclear Test Ban Treaty was her husband's most important accomplishment.

22 November 1963, the Kennedys arrive in Dallas, Texas

JACKIE

To prepare for his as yet unannounced presidential campaign of 1964, the president, accompanied by Jackie, flew to Texas for a two-day, five-city swing through the state. Texas was a must-win state if they were to stay in the White House for another term. This would be Jackie's first extended public appearance since the couple lost their premature two-day-old son Patrick to hyaline membrane disease in August 1963. This was the second time the couple had experienced excruciating sadness at the loss of a child. Before Caroline was born, a baby girl was stillborn. Both are buried near their mother and father in Arlington National Cemetery.

November 1963, Lyndon B. Johnson being sworn in as the new US president by Federal District Judge Sarah T. Hughes aboard the Presidential plane as his wife Lady Bird, former First Lady Jacqueline Kennedy, and others look on

JACKIE

In the midst of great personal despair and loss after her husband's assassination, Jackie rallied with a sole purpose: to memorialize him with dignity and to lead Americans in grieving for the loss of a popular president. As knowledgeable of history as she was, Jackie turned to the precedent of Abraham Lincoln's state funeral following his assassination 100 years earlier. Her sadness was palpable to all who watched the three days of proceedings, on television or in person. On the day his father was buried, 25 November 1963, John, Jr., turned three years old. At the urging of his mother, he solemnly saluted as his father's casket left the Cathedral of St. Matthew the Apostle where the funeral was held to make its way to Arlington National Cemetery.

25 November 1963, after receiving the American flag from her husband's casket

JACKIE

At her request, a week after her husband's death, Jackie invited Theodore White to visit her at the Kennedy compound in Hyannis Port so that she could recall for the historical record precious memories of her husband. During the four hours that she spoke to him, it was she who alluded to Camelot as capturing the magic of the Kennedy White House. She told White of how her husband listened to the music from the Broadway play of the same name, particularly enamored of the very last lines on the record: "Don't let it be forgot, that once there was a spot, for one brief shining moment, that was known as Camelot." Her choice of metaphor has stood the test of time.

25 November 1963, leaving the US Capitol with Caroline and John, Jr., and her brother-in-law, Attorney General Robert F. Kennedy, during President Kennedy's state funeral

JACKIE

After her husband's assassination, Jackie left Washington, DC, and moved to New York City. Steeped in her love of horses and the equestrian life, she eventually rented as a weekend getaway, a small farm in the Somerset Hills of New Jersey about an hour from Manhattan, where she and her children lived during the week. Ten years later, she made it permanent, purchasing the 10-acre estate in Bernardsville, New Jersey, at the heart of the state's horse and fox hunting country. The Peapack house as it was called was a comfortable yellow house with white trim. The walls of the main living spaces of the house were also painted a cheery yellow. Jackie owned the house until her death. It has now been torn down.

1966, between events at the St. Bernard's school horse show in Gladstone, New Jersey

JACKIE

As the president's widow, Jackie devoted her time to collaborating on the creation and development of the John F. Kennedy Library and participated in the academic direction of the Kennedy School of Government at Harvard University, her husband's alma mater. Her other causes included the revitalization of Pennsylvania Avenue in Washington, DC, and the placement of the Temple of Dendur, a gift of the Egyptian government during the Kennedy administration, in the Metropolitan Museum of Art situated across Fifth Avenue from her co-op apartment. Her efforts to salvage historical architecture extended to Venice, Italy, where she threw her sizeable global clout behind saving the city from rising water levels.

1966, being escorted by Nathan M. Pusey, president of Harvard University, to the dinner celebrating the new Institute of Politics at the John Fitzgerald Kennedy School of Government at Harvard

JACKIE

Out of the White House but not the limelight, Jackie continued to capture the imagination of the American public. In 1964, Andy Warhol unveiled his acrylic and silkscreen composition of nine identical images of the former first lady. The smiling photo of her was eerily captured just before tragedy struck in Dallas. In 1965, Jackie was named to the International Best Dressed Hall of Fame. For her wedding to Aristotle Onassis in October 1968, she wore a short lace and georgette dress by Valentino. Thereafter, Jackie was known the world over as simply Jackie O.

1967, with Irish Premier Jack Lynch in Ireland

JACKIE

I n 1967, Jackie made several notable trips abroad. One was a goodwill trip to Cambodia on which she was accompanied by the British widower David Ormsby Gore, Lord Harlech, a rumored romantic interest of Jackie. Over a three-day period they toured the ruins of the 12th-century Buddhist temple of Angkor Wat, the largest religious monument in the world. Earlier that year, Jackie vacationed with Caroline and John in Ireland where they visited Dungannon in County Wexford, from where their great-great-grandfather Patrick Joseph Kennedy had emigrated to America in 1858. The family was received enthusiastically. The house that Jackie and Jack built in the Virginia hunt country was named to honor the American Kennedy's Irish origin.

*1968, leaving a church in Palenque,
Mexico, with Roswell Gilpatric to whom
she was briefly romantically linked*

JACKIE

When Jack's brother Bobby decided to pursue the Democratic nomination for president in 1968, Jackie was both excited for him and concerned that he would befall the same fate as his brother. Three months after he threw his hat into the ring, Bobby was shot and killed in the kitchen of the Ambassador Hotel in Los Angeles. He had just won the crucial California primary that would likely have propelled him into the White House. In the mid-1960s Jackie was courted by many an eligible bachelor, one of whom was Aristotle Onassis. Bobby's death scared and saddened her, likely hastening her decision to accept Ari's marriage proposal.

1969, attending the broadway musical
Forty Carats *with architect Edward Barnes,*
a friend

JACKIE

On 20 October 1968 Jackie married Aristotle Onassis, an extremely wealthy Greek shipping tycoon, on the Greek island of Skorpios, which was owned by Onassis. Her choice of Onassis was very controversial, but he offered security and protection to her and to her children during unsettled times. Until Onassis' death in 1975, she made her home between New York City and Paris, the island of Skorpios and Onassis' 325-foot yacht, *The Christina*, named after his daughter, and her New Jersey farm.

20 October 1968, Jackie married Aristotle Socrates Onassis on Skorpios, Onassis's private island in the Ionian Sea.

JACKIE

The Onassis marriage shared a number of parallels with Jackie's marriage to Jack Kennedy. Both were wealthy, charismatic, commanding older men who pursued their chosen career with determination and passion. Each found in Jackie a partner who enhanced the whole through her sophistication, style, intelligence, and glamor. Both benefited by her presence in their public and professional lives. Ari's children, Alexander and Christina, were not fond of their stepmother Jackie, but Ari was kind and welcoming to her children. Alexander was killed in 1973 in a plane crash. Two years later Ari followed him in death, hastened perhaps by the loss of his son.

1970, walking through Rome's Leonardo da Vinci Airport as she was traveling from New York to Athens

JACKIE

After the more sedate and traditional clothing that she favored as political wife and First Lady, Jackie adopted pantsuits, silk head scarves, mini-skirts, and large, round, dark sunglasses for her life post–White House. She even appeared in public in jeans, launching the classic combination of white jeans and black top, never tucked in, sometimes a tee shirt and sometimes a turtleneck. This look endures today and appears every bit as fresh now as it did when she originated it in the 1970s.

1970, in Capri, Italy

JACKIE

After Aristotle Onassis, Jackie's second husband, died in 1975, she joined Viking Press in Manhattan as an editor. She quickly moved to the publishing house Doubleday, where she remained until her death in 1994. Her lifelong love of books, reading, and the quest for knowledge led her to publishing and kept her there. Ironically, she spent more years in this profession than as the wife of both a US president and of a Greek shipping magnate, yet the public knows so little about her life in this role. She was responsible for securing Michael Jackson's memoir, *Moonwalk,* as well as the ballerina Gelsey Kirkland's autobiography, *Dancing on My Grave.* Mirroring her affection for Paris, she also brought *Unseen Versailles* to the world's bookshelves.

1970, in Capri, Italy, with the fashion designer Valentino

JACKIE

In the last years of her marriage to Onassis, Jackie was aware that he was attempting to divorce her. He died before the subject of divorce could be broached. Because she was not Greek, Jackie could not inherit. A year after Ari's death, in 1976, she and her stepdaughter Christina agreed on a $26 million settlement from the Onassis estate. Jackie never married again but she did enjoy a stable, contented relationship with Maurice Tempelsman that lasted longer than either of her marriages. Tempelsman would be by her side in 1994 when she died.

1970, attending a gala performance of ballet and opera honoring impresario Sol Hurok, with George Moore of the Metropolitan Opera Association

JACKIE

Throughout her life, Jackie remained a subject of intense media scrutiny and the person most obsessed with her was the paparazzo Ron Galella. He surprised her at every turn as she pursued her daily activities in New York City, but he didn't stop there. He followed her around the world attempting to capture the Jackie that no one ever saw. His presence became so problematic to her that in 1972 she sought and won an injunction against him, but that was only a temporary fix. They would be back in court again.

*March 1972, arriving at New York's Federal Court to seek
an injunction prohibiting paparazzo Ron Galella from
coming within 100 yards of her*

JACKIE

Numerous accolades and honors, both during her lifetime and posthumously, have been given to Jackie. The main reservoir in Central Park, around which she frequently biked or jogged, was renamed the Jacqueline Kennedy Onassis Reservoir. In tribute to her tireless work on behalf of the Municipal Art Society of New York to save New York City's magnificent architecture, especially Grand Central Station, the organization presents a medal named in her honor to an individual whose efforts have made an outstanding contribution to the city. A dormitory at George Washington University was named for the school's famous alumna. And quite suitably, the East Garden at the White House is named the Jacqueline Kennedy Garden.

June 1975, with her daughter, Caroline, and Rose Kennedy at Caroline's graduation from Concord Academy in Concord, Massachusetts

JACKIE

Jacqueline Bouvier Kennedy Onassis died all too soon at the age of 64 on 19 May 1994 in her Fifth Avenue apartment surrounded by family. In January of the same year she had been diagnosed with non-Hodgkin's lymphoma, a form of cancer of the lymphatic system. During her illness, she maintained her work schedule and social activities, greeting her fate with the grace and majesty that the world had come to expect of her. She was buried next to her first husband President John F. Kennedy in Arlington National Cemetery near Washington, DC, guarded by the eternal flame.

March 1975, leaving her New York apartment building
after being recently widowed for a second time

Gravesite of President John F. Kennedy and his wife, Jacqueline, at Arlington National Cemetery near Washington, DC